THE SELF AND THE OTHER

THE SELF AND THE OTHER

Personhood and Images among the Baule, Côte d'Ivoire

Philip L. Ravenhill

Fowler Museum of Cultural History
University of California, Los Angeles

Monograph Series Number 28

This catalogue and associated exhibition
were supported by funding from the following:

The Ahmanson Foundation
The National Endowment for the Humanities Challenge Grant
The Times Mirror Foundation
Manus, the Support Group of the UCLA Fowler Museum of Cultural History

Front Cover: Detail and alternative view of Figure 6, page 12.
Page 1: Detail of Figure 10, page 16.
Page 2: Detail of Figure 1, page 8.
Page 3: Alternative view of Figure 41, page 38.
Page 6: Alternative view of Figure 7, page 13.
Page 48: Alternative view of Figure 42, page 38.
Back cover: Alternative views of Figures 21, 42, 17, 53, and 15.

Fowler Museum of Cultural History
University of California, Los Angeles
405 Hilgard Avenue
Los Angeles, California, USA 90024-1549

Printed and bound in Hong Kong
by Pearl River Printing Company, Ltd.

ISBN 0-930741-39-0

Library of Congress Catalog Card Number: 94-70815

Location of the Baule

Acknowledgments

This monograph and accompanying exhibition began as one of the inspired focus gallery projects that the National Museum of African Art has so effectively mounted over the past five years. I would like to thank Sylvia Williams, director of the museum, for allowing us to share the resources and ideas of *Dreaming the Other World: Figurative Art of the Baule, Côte d'Ivoire.*

Dr. Philip Ravenhill, Chief Curator of the National Museum of African Art organized both exhibitions with great sensitivity and insight. Few scholars in the fields of African art history and anthropology inspire the profound perceptions of African culture that are so characteristic of Philip's research. Working under unreasonable deadlines, he constantly responded on time and with good humor. I am extremely grateful for his considerable and thoughtful efforts on our behalf.

The UCLA version of the exhibition was expanded with key loans from local collectors. I would especially like to thank: Richard and Jan Baum, Geraldine and Morton Dimondstein, Jerome L. Joss, Saul and Marsha Stanhoff, Judith Timyan, and Dr. and Mrs. Leon Wallace

In addition, the University of Iowa Museum of Art agreed to lend a key figure to the exhibition. I sincerely appreciate the extra efforts of Chris Roy and JoAnn Conklin in facilitating the loan.

This monograph was designed by the Fowler Museum's Director of Publications Daniel Brauer with typical flair and a keen appreciation for the objects. The photography was handled with considerable sensitivity by Denis Nervig. Irina Averkieff edited the manuscript with intelligence and care. The remaining details were handled by Elisabeth Cameron, my research assistant and colleague for the past two years. The remainder of the museum staff, listed at the back of the volume, performed with characteristic excellence. It is always a joy to work with such professionals.

Doran H. Ross
Deputy Director

Research on Baule figurative art was first undertaken in 1976–77 while I was engaged in a study of the Goli masquerade that was supported by a grant from the Wenner-Gren Foundation for anthropological research. I continued to work on Baule art while I was a researcher employed by the Institut d'Histoire, d'Art, et d'Archéologie africains (IHAAA) of the Université d'Abidjan from 1977 to 1982. In 1993 I explored Baule art in an exhibition, *Dreaming the Other World: Figurative Art of the Baule, Côte d'Ivoire*, at the National Museum of African Art. The assistance of all three institutions is gratefully acknowledged.

My original publication on Baule figurative art (Ravenhill 1980) benefited from a close reading by Susan Vogel, and my debt to her ongoing research on the Baule is apparent. I would also like to thank Judith Timyan for her collaboration in the exegesis of Baule concepts and in their proper transcription. Finally I would like to express my appreciation to the staff of the Fowler Museum for their fruitful collaboration in this publication and the exhibition it accompanies. Particular thanks are due to Doran Ross, deputy director, for his invitation to undertake this endeavor and his ongoing encouragement to my musings on the meanings of African art. Irina Averkieff, with grace and humor, has brought her editorial skill to bear on the present text. Daniel R. Brauer deserves special thanks for his excellent design work accomplished in record time.

Philip L. Ravenhill
June, 1994

1. STANDING MALE FIGURE

Collected in the Dimbokro region of Côte d'Ivoire in 1947. Wood and metal. Height: 45 cm. Collection of Judith Timyan.

2. STANDING FEMALE FIGURE

Wood and paint. Height: 40 cm. FMCH 94.17.5. Anonymous gift. *(Profile view may be found on page 20.)*

3. STANDING MALE FIGURE

Wood and paint. Height: 24.4 cm. National Museum of African Art, Smithsonian Institution. Anonymous gift.

4. STANDING FEMALE FIGURE

Wood, beads, thread, and metal. Height: 38.5 cm. Collection of Dr. and Mrs. Leon Wallace.

The Baule of central Côte d'Ivoire[1] refer to their sculpted figures as *waka sran*. *Waka* means wood and *sran* means person, so the compound term can readily be translated into English as "wood(en) person." Each figure portrays human features. But, more important, each figure very much represents a "person."

This essay explores Baule notions of personhood as they relate to the carved images *(waka sran)* that are created either as intermediaries to the spirits of the natural world known as *asiɛ usu* (literally, "earth-spirits") or to the individual spirit mate of the opposite sex that each human has in the "Other World" *(blɔlɔ)*. The fundamental question I want to raise is: Why are these invisible, supernatural forces conceived and represented by the Baule as human beings *(sran mu)*?

The Self and the Other

Introduction

The Baule peoples live in the central region of Côte d'Ivoire, West Africa; their language is related to the Akan language of Ghana. They live mainly in the savanna region between the Bandama and N'Zi rivers (see map, page 5), although many have migrated to forested areas in the south to grow coffee and cocoa or are now settled in towns and cities such as Bouaké and Abidjan.

In the past, the Baule were subsistence farmers and hunters; artists and artisans usually practiced their crafts in their spare time. Yet Baule artists have produced numerous examples of many different types of art. They are famous for finely sculpted face masks; carved wood figures; cast gold and copper jewelry and other objects; prestige items, such as staffs or flywhisks carved in wood and covered with gold foil; carved pulleys for looms; wood chairs, stools, and headrests; and sculpted door panels. They have also carved ivory bracelets, combs, and side-blown trumpets.

Works of art from the Baule region are considered to form a style that is separate and distinct from other Ivorian cultures. Specific categories of Baule art are, however, related both by history and style to the art forms of neighboring groups. The art of goldworking is related to that of the Akan of Ghana. Some masks forms have been borrowed from Mande groups to the west. Figurative art is related to

5. STANDING MALE FIGURE
Wood. Height: 35 cm. Collection of Richard and Jan Baum.

the art of the Wan and Guro. Weaving and indigo-dyeing are linked to groups to the west and north.

Baule artistic creation has taken place within a richly textured history of exchange and inspiration. Each work of art has been created in response to a need, whether practical, aesthetic, or existential — a need, that is, for things to be different.

The Baule Worldview: Community and Personhood

To date, the best attempt at understanding and translating the profound complexities of Baule thought and cultural practice is found in the collected work of Pierre Étienne, a French anthropologist who worked among the Baule from 1962 until his death in 1975.[2] His important text "Le fait villageois Baoulé" (1976) presents a sympathetic, phenomenological understanding of Baule concepts of culture, nature, and the supernatural, which allows a deep appreciation of Baule ways of being and doing. It is upon Étienne's ground-breaking work that the present inquiry is based.

Let us begin our look at Baule culture by examining the meaning of community. What defines communal life? What does it mean to be "human" *(sran)* for the Baule? What are some of the constitutive rules that determine correct behavior and govern interpersonal expectations and interactions? I choose to begin this exploration by reflecting upon a phrase I overheard many years ago when I was first starting fieldwork among the Baule: *Ɔ ti a sran!* "He is not a person!" Since this phrase was uttered about someone whom I, at least, perceived to be a normal human, I realized that the phrase had to imply some criteria of judgment in terms of which the man in question had come up short. Expectations had not been met. Apparently, the man could not be counted on to act according to fundamental rules governing correct behavior, reciprocity, and communal life. Thus he was either a flouter of social norms or he was unpredictable, but in either case he was seen as placing himself outside of the rules governing life lived in the community and therefore "not a human."

Another common utterance that one hears often in Baule villages is the question: *N ti a sran?* "Am I not a person?" Most often, this question-*cum*-statement is hurled rhetorically as a challenge to someone who has totally failed to take into account another's presence — to someone who has failed to acknowledge and formally recognize by a proper greeting the company, indeed, the existence of another human being.

From the point of view of American society, where greetings are often minimal ("Hi!"), or completely nonverbal (upraised eyebrows or a slight movement of the head), how can one begin to understand the complexities and underlying realities of a formal system of greetings such as that of the Baule? Among them there are greetings that differentiate men from women, old from young, that differ depending on the time of day (morning, noon, afternoon, and evening), that recognize an activity that is under way (*Nja mo o,* "Men, thank you for the work"), that acknowledge someone's return from the fields, that remember the previous encounter or exchange (*Anuman kwlao,* "Thank you for [the good you did me] yesterday"), that acknowledge the extended family, or that recognize that since the previous encounter a child has been born or a relative has died. The exchange of greetings may sometimes seem formulaic and predictable to the outsider, but any failure to initiate the exchange is perceived as a most profound insult: "Am *I* not a person?" *N ti a sran?*

It is through each exchange of greetings that awareness of the other person's active and evolving presence in the world is acknowledged. Changes in social identity (parenthood, widowhood, return from a long sojourn "elsewhere") are formally recognized through such greetings, and thus a lively ongoing relationship is maintained. For the Baule, Guerry says "The beautiful is equivalent to the good, and the summit of perfection is to jealously maintain the links that unite us to others" (1972:37).

The *sine qua non* of Baule social life is the fact that all participants have a fundamental equivalence: Each is

6. *(Left) STANDING FEMALE FIGURE AND SEATED MALE FIGURE*

Female: Wood. Height: 45.7 cm.
FMCH 67.2033B. *Gift of George G. Frelinghuysen.*
Male: Wood. Height: 48.3 cm.
FMCH 67.2033A. *Gift of George G. Frelinghuysen.*

(Detail views may be found on page 32.)

7. *(Right) SEATED FEMALE FIGURE*

Wood. Height: 45 cm.
Collection of Dr. and Mrs. Leon Wallace.

(Profile view may be found on page 6.)

inescapably a "human" *(sran)*, and, as such, governed by the same laws of shared community. This is the starting point that makes communal life possible. The rules are clear: You acknowledge me, and I will acknowledge you. This may seem prickly and standoffish, a defensive or perhaps paranoid position from which to begin any interactive process, yet it does serve to establish a minimal platform upon which subsequent exchanges can occur. In recognizing you through a greeting, thereby making a formal acknowledgment of your existence, a common bond is established: We are like beings — communication is possible, human interaction can occur.

It is easy for the outsider, especially the non-African, to fail to appreciate the fundamental importance of speech in Baule culture. Following de Saussure, we may believe that it is only language that is rule-governed. Speech can be thought of as nothing more than the accidental utterance of grammar. We may fail to acknowledge the importance of speech in the social construction of reality and the maintenance of social relationships. A non-African would choose to define these relationships otherwise: by pre-established roles, for example, or by power politics. But what of relationships that *only* exist through speech? Consider the infamous "joking relationship" from anthropological literature. How can the existential reality of an affective relationship, such as the Baule joking relationship known as *tukpɛ*,[3] which exists only through speech, be properly understood? Such a relationship has virtually no other reality than the process of verbal exchange. The gap between the Western use of language, so heavily dependent on the importance and propositional content of the written word, and spoken speech in Baule society, where each participant is keenly aware of the nuance of every performative utterance, is profound.

Public speech (words spoken in front of someone who, if need be, can bear witness) and formal speech (the performative utterances of sworn oaths, declarations, benedictions, or curses) are seen and judged by Baule as actions — events with consequences. The revelatory speech of divination is a particular kind of public speech; its goal is to disclose hidden causes, to establish heretofore hidden truths, and to reveal possible solutions to the crisis that led to the divination session.

The Supernatural, Nature, and Culture

For the Baule, a hidden world of supernatural causality lies behind the events and crises of human existence. Sickness, misfortune, and personal failure are due to hidden spiritual causes. To find out why something has happened and how resolution can be effected, one needs to consult a diviner (*wunnzueyifwɛ*, "revealer of causes").

The most common form of divination among the Baule is *ngɔinman*. The *ngɔinman* diviner, always a man (to the best of my knowledge), manipulates nine leather thongs on each of which is knotted a specific object — various forms and kinds of metals (iron and brass), and body parts of animals (a scale from a pangolin, the hoof of a particular duiker, the tooth of a leopard), representing either a social actor (adult man, young man, adult woman, young woman) or a metaphysical concept (fire, thing, movement, mouth/speech). The nine thongs are jumbled together, beaten against a leather pad, then covered by the diviner's hand and repetitively extracted three by three in "message-units" that are interpreted in concert with an evolving dialogue that occurs between the diviner, the client(s), and family members. A combination of "young man," "young woman," and "fire" can be interpreted, for example, as indicative of secret adultery, depending, of course, on what is actually being said by those who have asked for the consultation.

8. STANDING MALE AND FEMALE FIGURES
Male: Wood. Height: 48.5 cm.
FMCH 86.1739. Promised gift of Jerome L. Joss.
Female: Wood. Height: 50 cm.
FMCH 86.1740. Promised gift of Jerome L. Joss.
(Back view may be found on page 32.)

9. (Right) The sculptor Koffi Nianmien with the figure of his Other-World woman. Toumodi region, Côte d'Ivoire, 1981. Photograph by Philip Ravenhill.

10. (Above) Woman with her husband and the figure of her Other-World man. Toumodi region, Côte d'Ivoire, 1981. Photograph by Philip Ravenhill.

11. (Right) Woman with her daughter and the figure of her Other-World man. Toumodi region, Côte d'Ivoire, 1981. Photograph by Philip Ravenhill.

Portraits

12. Woman with the figure of her Other-World man and her husband with the figure of his Other-World woman. Toumodi region, Côte d'Ivoire, 1981. Photograph by Philip Ravenhill.

Where does the revealed knowledge come from? What other reality subtends physical reality? Behind the reality of village life, beyond the realm of culture, what powers are active in the world? For the Baule, there are two other realms of existence: nature and the supernatural. Étienne has said of the Baule:

> I would be rather tempted to say that, for them, all of nature is supernatural and that every supernatural phenomenon participates in nature to different degrees. As for culture, a product of human activity, it derives from both realities. There is no practical human activity which does not implicate, or which does not refer to, a supernatural context (1976:30).

At a fundamental level, nature is seen as Earth *(asiɛ)*, the essential power with whom an alliance has been established, which allows man to take over a part of nature's domain, establish a village, and to work and profit from the land. Every Baule village has been founded by a *takafwɛ*,[4] the one who "called *(taka)* the earth" in order to create the alliance that guarantees the existence of village society (Étienne 1976:33, n. 19). "Earth is a fetish *(amuin)* that one possesses, that one transmits to one's inheritors" (Guerry 1972:102), and thus there are rules that ensure that this relationship is properly maintained and mutually beneficial. On certain days of the week (Monday and/or Wednesday and/or Friday, depending on the region), no field labor can be undertaken lest the Earth be "spoiled" *(ɔ'a saki)*. Similarly, the Earth can be spoiled if human sexual activity takes place outside the village proper. Earth is the underlying reality and power that enforces the rules of culture; it is a constant reminder that life in culture, the village *(klɔ)*, is different from life beyond the village edge, in the natural world of the bush *(blo)*. Earth, Étienne has argued,

> is less an object for appropriation than the partner in an alliance. In exchange for the services of its cult and respect for interdictions on work or sexual activity, it gives people abundant harvests and protects them from the evil intentions and actions of its savage denizens and from accidents (1976:39).

Human society as a collectivity, the village, is defined in relation to Earth.

> It is only when Earth has accepted propitiatory sacrifices, has accepted that people can engage in sexual activity on its land, [and] that the alliance has been sealed by the implantation in an encampment of the tree and stone for *asiɛ*, it is only then that man can live a fully human existence (Étienne 1976:42).

Earth has a primordial and perdurable identity that differentiates it from all of the other fetishes also associated with the natural world.

> It is difficult...to define the nature of *amuin*. There is no doubt that they belong to the supernatural realm. But one is not aware of their universe, their true world. Certainly, one can be familiar with the material support of their being, of their power (mask, statues, bracelets and amulets, shrines, etc.) that one can call *(taka)* to the village to ask for protection or to offer them sacrifices. But one does not know where they "live".... In fact, they are everywhere and it is only by appropriate rituals that one can fix their presence in a mask, a statue in clay, etc. (Étienne 1976:33).

13. STANDING MALE AND FEMALE FIGURES
Male: Wood and cloth. Height: 43.4 cm.
FMCH 87.1213. Gift of Jerome L. Joss.
Female: Wood, cloth, and beads. Height: 42.5 cm.
FMCH 87.1463. Gift of Jerome L. Joss.

Pairs

When a male and a female figure are recognized as having been carved by the same artist, demonstrate comparable patterns of wear and use, and have the same collection history, it can be assumed that the figures probably represent *asiɛ usu* spirits and were used together by a trance diviner *(komiɛn)*. It should also be noted, however, that male and female figures by the same artist may *not* have been created as a pair; they may have been carved contemporaneously as representatives of Other-World mates for a man and a woman in the same village or region, but have been collected separately by an African dealer, only becoming a "pair" through his agency.

14. (Far left) STANDING FEMALE FIGURE

Wood and paint. Height: 30 cm.

FMCH 94.17.2. Anonymous gift.

(Detail view may be found on page 43.)

15. (Left) STANDING MALE FIGURE

Wood and paint. Height: 30 cm.

FMCH 94.17.3. Anonymous gift.

(Detail view may be found on page 42.)

16. (Right) STANDING MALE FIGURE

Wood and paint. Height: 34 cm.

FMCH 94.18.2. Anonymous gift.

17. (Far right) STANDING FEMALE FIGURE

Wood and paint. Height: 40 cm.

FMCH 94.17.5. Anonymous gift.

(Alternative view may be found on page 8.)

MacGaffey (1990), cross-referencing Pietz (1985), has argued that "The problem of the fetish, for the European mind, has been that it confounds the distinction, regarded as basic and natural, between objects and persons." The term "fetish" has largely gone out of favor — as in the use of "power object" for the former "nail fetish" of the Kongo — and often evokes embarrassment, as though the outside scholar was being pejorative in his description. Yet the term is useful when properly explained according to a specific "local theory of powerful and disturbing experiences" (MacGaffey 1990:58). For the Baule, the relevant features of *amuin* are that they are supernatural forces that can be called upon and that their powers can be usefully channeled when given a material support. It is important to understand the distinction that the Baule make between the existence of the *amuin* itself and the material *thing* in which its power is ultimately captured. The material form of the fetish is called *amuin ba* by the Baule; the basic sense of *ba* is "child" or the "young" of an animal, but it is also used in the sense of "unit" or "part of a larger whole"; thus *amuin ba* can be glossed as the "fetish entity." Once localized, it is the "thingness" of the *amuin* that predominates. It is because the "fetish" is a "thing" that it can be appropriated, acquired, transported, and used; it is a proprietary power that can be ordered about.

> The adept is the owner of his fetish. He has no respect for him; his prayer often resembles bargaining: "If you give me a good harvest, you will have a goat." ...and when he is not satisfied with his services, he uses blackmail: "Attention! I am going to drop you and find another fetish." ...If the fetish is ineffective, one menaces it, insults it, and finally can throw it away in the bush (Guerry 1972:106).

Of a different order of supernatural entities are the special spirits known as *asiɛ usu* (literally, "earth-spirits") which inhabit certain features of the natural world: hills,

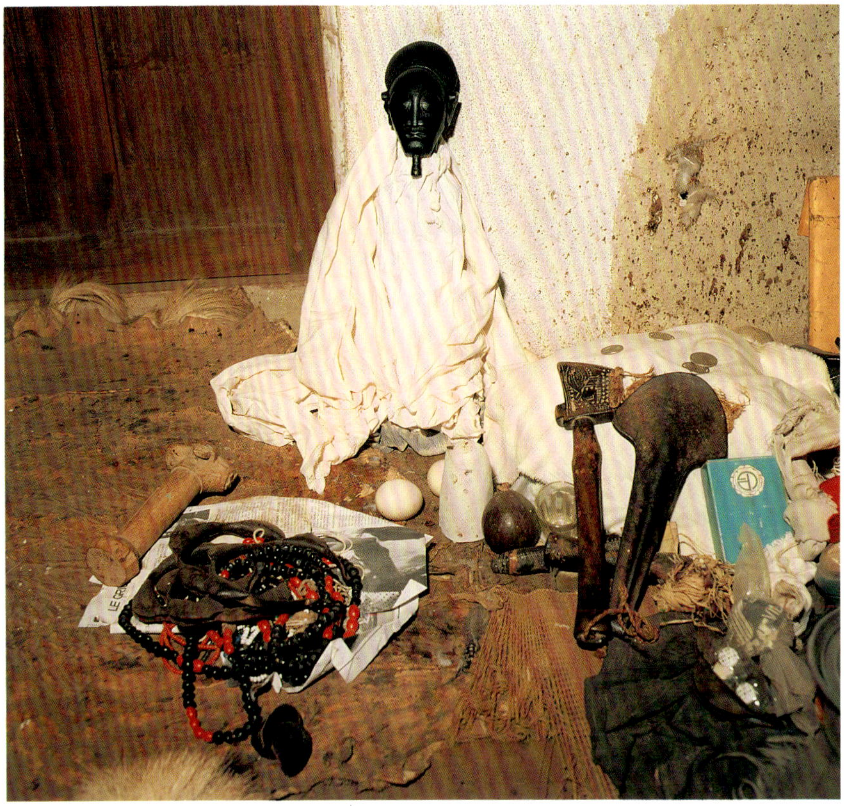

18. *(Left)* Komiɛn *diviner. Toumodi region, Côte d'Ivoire. 1981. Photograph by Philip Ravenhill.*

19. *(Right) Figure representing the* asiɛ usu *of the* komiɛn *diviner with her gong* (lawre) *and gong-beater* (lawre waka). *Toumodi region, Côte d'Ivoire. 1981. Photograph by Lap Nguyen Tien.*

mountains, rocks, water sources, rivers, and some plants. These spirits, which may at times take on human form (Figs. 13 and 19) and be seen, are of a quite different ontological status than the *amuin*.

> While it is men who discover *amuin*, who call them, who force them to come to the village (e.g., as masks) or install them there, ... it is the *asie usu* which come to men, it is they who take the initiative to make contact with men; they follow them, they importune them, they seize them, they cause them to enter trances during which the one possessed by the *asie usu* becomes "clairvoyant" and can prophesy (Guerry 1972:37).

Just as the alliance with a fetish *(amuin)* is a source of power, either protective or destructive, so too contact with *asie usu* may produce in human beings such extraordinary effects as clairvoyance or madness. *Asiɛ usu* may choose to initiate a relationship with a person and forge an alliance that links him or her to some of the powers inherent in nature. If the chosen person agrees to and appropriately formalizes the relationship, he or she may become a clairvoyant *(komiɛnfwɛ*, or simply *komiɛn)* who prophesies in trance (Fig. 18), that is, a "prophet" *(awɛfwɛ)*, "one who uses the frontiers *(ɔ di awɛ)*, who wanders in the no man's land that separates the world of man from that of the gods" (Guerry 1972:106). His or her relationship to the *asiɛ usu* is formalized by the commissioning, sculpting, and installing of a figure that symbolizes the fact that henceforth the spirit will also live within the confines of the village. When the *asiɛ usu* "mounts" his partner — in the same way that a person mounts a horse — he takes charge, and the person in trance is empowered to see things that are otherwise unseen and to pronounce truths that are otherwise hidden. The *komiɛn* maintains his relationship to his *asiɛ usu* by placing offerings in a small pottery bowl at the feet of the figure. The figure is also displayed during public performances, a sign of contact

20. MOUSE ORACLE
Ceramic, metal, cord, leather, and plant fiber. Height of container: 16 cm. FMCH 84.1060.

with the powers of the natural world beyond the village boundary — an acknowledged outside presence that changes received realities.

The Supernatural World and Divination

The powers of the supernatural world found in nature impinge on the human world and cause things to happen; they can also serve to explain events and states of human experience and reveal hidden knowledge. The "revealer of causes" *(wunnzueyifwɛ)* is able to make his revelations because of his contact with the supernatural world. The most striking and dramatic means of divination is the public performance of the *komiɛnfwɛ*, whose power, as we have seen, is derived from contact with the *asiɛ usu*. Other diviners also explore the hidden realm and it is thought that they, too, make contact with the extraordinary powers of Earth and nature.

As discussed earlier, the most common method of divination for the Baule is *ngɔinman,* which involves the use of nine symbol-laden leather cords. Another method is the use of a "mouse oracle" *(glekle sɛ)*, a two-chambered container made of wood or clay in which a mouse lives (Figs. 20 and 21). The mouse hides in the lower chamber and comes to the upper chamber when the diviner inserts rice chaff and closes the clay lid. In eating, the mouse rearranges the positions of small beaded or bone shafts attached to a small tray (of either brass or a tortoise carapace). The new arrangement of these elements is read by the diviner and interpreted, like the *ngɔinman*, according to the dialogue with his client(s). The power of the mouse oracle, it was explained to me, lies in the fact that the mouse, via a small hole in the lower chamber that permits the evacuation of urine and excrement, is in direct contact with the Earth. *Awa*, a small, bowl-like gourd filled with water, is also used as a divination tool, as is a small hand mirror.

In contradistinction to the public drama of the performance of the *komiɛnfwɛ* stand the more personal sessions of consultation that center on a diviner and his or her divinatory instrument of choice. Here, the emphasis is on speech and verbal exchange. The divining tool is like the rudder of a boat; held against the flow of discourse, it directs onward movement. In the hands and through the eyes of the diviner, the instrument is exceedingly "context sensitive": it confirms or denies what is being asserted, opens up new avenues of inquiry, and closes down others. All present, husband and wife and their respective (extended) families, can weigh in, ask a question, make a comment, react in surprise or affirmation to the words of the diviner: "Can it be because I did (or didn't!) do this?"

The divination process, one which may necessitate many sessions and one that totally involves all participants, leads ultimately to the establishment of a conclusion — a revelation that all agree to. The final revelation becomes a matter of consensus. Admitted by all, perceived to be the revealed truth, the conclusion establishes a new way of understanding the exigencies of personal experience, and henceforth all agree to the explanation of a new reality heretofore hidden. Such is the nature of divination in Baule life.

The Other World

In addition to the realms of the village (culture) and the bush (nature), the Baule also believe in a far-off place that they call *blɔlɔ* (pronounced *'blaw·law)*. It is a place "which exists beyond sensory experience" (Étienne 1976:30). According to Baule tradition, the word is derived from the phrase *be blɔ lɔ*, "they recount things about that place" or "they vaunt, or brag about, that place." The sense of the morpheme *lɔ* is "over-there, in the sense of the far-off, the distanced" (Étienne1976). *Blɔlɔ* can thus be translated as "the place that is bragged about." It is the "Beyond" or "Other World" that exists through boastful recounting. It is always "there" and never "here."

The Other World is thought of as an ideal world, a place of exaggerated perfection. It is also called

> "the village of truth," in opposition to the village on earth, to this world of appearances where one never knows the basis of things, where people live in

21. *MOUSE ORACLE*

Ceramic, wood, and metal. Height of container: 14 cm. Length of longest tray: 10 cm. FMCH 94.19.1. *Anonymous gift.*

22. MINIATURE FIGURES

Figures of Other-World mates worn on beaded necklaces. Shown actual size. Height of tallest: 10 cm. Left to right: FMCH 94.13.2, FMCH 94.13.1, FMCH 94.13.6. All anonymous gifts.

> untruth and deceive each other. When one enters this universe [of the *blɔlɔ*], one sees the true sense of things, and no one can any longer deceive you (Guerry 1972:90).

The *blɔlɔ* is inhabited by human spirits; it is the place from which comes the spirit of a newborn and the place to which a person's spirit returns at death. It is also a place where each person has a partner of the opposite sex. A woman has an "Other-World man" *(blɔlɔ bian)*; a man has an "Other-World woman" *(blɔlɔ bla)*.[5]

A person's Other-World mate may make his or her existence known and demand recognition by creating a problem, often one that relates to marriage, sexuality, or childbearing. It is in consulting a diviner about the hidden cause of the problem that it may be revealed that the cause is the jealousy of the Other-World mate. The diviner may recommend that his or her existence be acknowledged by having a figure[6] carved. Figures are usually 10 to 15 inches (25 to 38 cm) in height, but in some regions the figures can be made very small and worn on a necklace; these figures, two to three inches (5 to 7.5 cm) in height, are eminently portable and personal (Figs. 22 and 23). The figure "brings down" or "creates" *(jra)* the invisible mate in tangible form. The person is now "here" as well as "there."

The Other-World mate is also acknowledged by the act of reserving one designated night of the week as a time for the mate to visit in dreams. Every week, on the same night, the person sleeps alone and dreams about the Other-World person. The following morning, the figure is addressed and small offerings are made. In this way, one establishes an ongoing relationship with the Other-World mate, and the problem that led to the commissioning and installation of the figure perhaps finds a resolution.

23. MINIATURE FIGURES

Figures of Other-World mates worn on beaded necklaces. Shown actual size. Height of tallest: 9.5 cm. Left to right: FMCH 94.13.3, anonymous gift; FMCH 94.13.4, collection of Judith Timyan; FMCH 94.13.5, anonymous gift.

Figurative Arts: The *Person* in Wood

Let us return to our opening challenge: Why are some invisible, supernatural forces conceived and represented by the Baule as human beings? Two quite different types of supernatural beings, *asiɛ usu* and the men and women of the *blɔlɔ*, are represented by sculptors in essentially the same way. Although they may be used and handled differently, both types of figures are conceived and created as miniature idealizations of human beauty.

Notions of Form

The key to appreciating the form of a Baule figure is to understand that the artist carves it according to the same standards of beauty that the society uses for evaluating the beauty of real people (cf. Ravenhill 1980, 1993; Vogel 1980). The figure is carved as a person *(sran)*, a "person in wood" *(waka sran)*. It is considered to idealize human beauty, and, like a human being, its physical attributes should be "just so" *(sɛsɛ)* — neither too pronounced nor too diminutive.

The emphasis and attention paid to the carving of the head and face of a figure are important for the portrayal of the physical identity of an individual person. The hair — a physical attribute that is always socially defined — is carefully depicted in a hairdo that calls attention to the presentation of self and also serves as a frame for the frontal

24. (Left) STANDING FEMALE FIGURE
Wood and pigment. Height: 38.1 cm.
FMCH 86.392. Anonymous gift.

25. (Right) SEATED MALE FIGURE AND STANDING FEMALE FIGURE
Wood. Height: (male) 36 cm, (female) 42 cm.
Collection of Geraldine and Morton Dimondstein.

26. (Below) Back view of Figure 25.

orientation and gaze of the face. Eyes are often depicted as downcast, perhaps to convey a sense of privacy. The nose, mouth, and ears are sharply delineated. The face usually imparts a sense of quiet dignity. Composure is also found in the hands that are at rest on the belly, the comfortable stance of a figure's flexed legs (Fig. 5), or the depiction of the figure as seated on a stool or chair (Fig. 25).

The neck is usually given great emphasis because the ideal neck for the Baule is quite long (Fig. 1). The general interpretation of the figure's body makes clear Baule ideas of bodily volume. Just as the head is set off from the body by the neck, so too is the trunk set off from the hips and legs by the pelvic circle. The pelvic circle is an important component of female beauty because an ample, rather than narrow, pelvic circle is a sign of childbearing potential — a potential confirmed by full breasts and a gently swelling belly (Fig. 27). Well-developed calf muscles are a sign of beauty for both men and women (Fig. 28).

In the past, scarification of the body was seen in terms of beauty — patterned textures that called attention to smooth skin (cf. Vogel 1988). On a figure, scarification is also a means of individuation. The individual depiction created by the artist is complemented by the owner's further personalization of the figure through the addition, for example, of a beaded necklace (perhaps with gold jewels), the different strings of beads that would have held up a loincloth around the hips, or beads below the knees or around the ankles.

27. (Left) STANDING FEMALE FIGURE
Wood. Height: 48.5 cm. Collection of Richard and Jan Baum.

28. (Right) STANDING FEMALE FIGURE
Wood. Height: 40 cm. FMCH 86.1112. Anonymous gift.
(Detail view may be found on page 33.)

29. (Far right) SEATED MALE FIGURE
Wood, cord, and cloth. Height: 43.5 cm.
Collection of Saul and Marsha Stanhoff.
(Detail views may be found on page 33.)

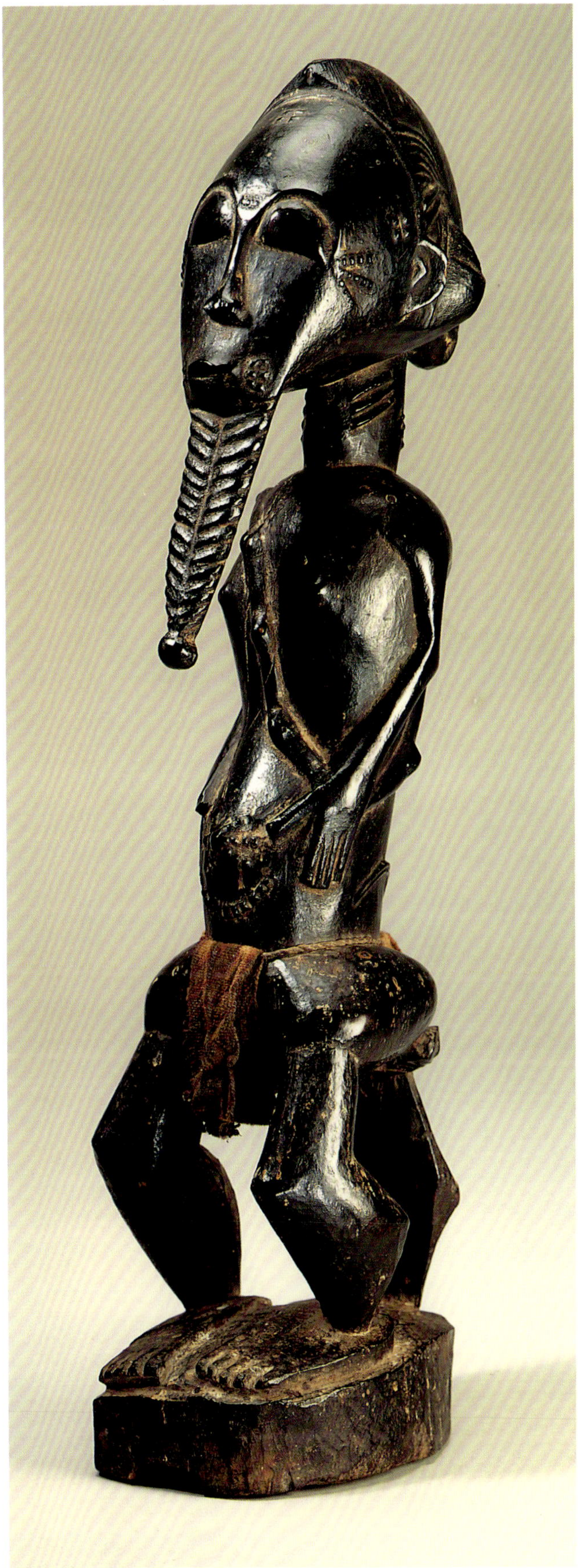

30. (Above, top) Detail of Figure 6, page 12.
31. (Above) Detail of Figure 6, page 12.

32. Back views of Figure 8, page 14.

33. Back view of Figure 29, page 31.

34. (Above, top) Detail of Figure 28, page 31.
35. (Above) Detail of Figure 29, page 31.

36. *(Left) The Other-World woman of the sculptor Koffi Niamnien next to a mound* (lo fannin) *of kaolin and an offering of eggs. Toumodi region, Côte d'Ivoire. 1981. Photograph by Lap Nguyen Tien.*

37. *(Right) and 38. (Far right) Figure of the Other-World woman of a wandering minstrel* (jitabofwɛ). *Toumodi region, Côte d'Ivoire. 1981. Photograph by Lap Nguyen Tien.*

Notions of Personhood

The figure carved by the sculptor only becomes an effective image when it is consecrated and "lodged" *(sike)* in the house of the person who commissioned it (Figs. 37 and 38). The "person in wood" *(waka sran)*, I would argue, is much like a human stranger who is received or lodged in one's home.

> The greatest respect is reserved for the stranger. ...[H]e is... the mediator par excellence, so why not reserve for him the greatest respect and the best welcome?
>
> In the house where he arrives, one must drink palm-wine in his honor. A bedroom is specially prepared for him.... In the morning, before his hostess leaves for the fields, his breakfast is already prepared for him. At meal times the message is sent to him "Your thing is over there," *O like o lɛ* (Effimbra 1959:204).

For the stranger, the neighbor or other village resident or, for that matter, any human being, social interaction begins and is governed by respect: "The Baule, in general are respectful; this is noted above all in the exchange of greetings" (Effimbra 1959:255). Respect is a constitutional condition of being human. Indeed, the equivalent term in Baule for the verb "respect" is "to think [of one] as human," as in *Ɔ bu mi sran*, "He respects me / he takes me seriously" (Carteron 1972:154), or literally, "He thinks of me as a human." It is interesting that for the Baule there is a funda-

mental equivalence between the person who is lodging and the person who is being lodged; both host and guest are referred to as *sikefwɛ*.

Am I overemphasizing the human *(sran)* aspect of the "wooden figure" *(waka sran)*? I think not, for the parallels are constant and consistent. Through the figure, the spirit — be it *asiɛ usu* or *blɔlɔ* man or woman — is "called" *(taka)*, is "greeted" *(yo...likɛ)*, is "lodged" *(sike)*, and is "fed" *(di aliɛ)* through offerings (Fig. 36). In brief, the spirit is treated with respect and is "thought of as a person." The spirit is perceived as an active person who volitionally initiates contact with a specific human being and demands recognition in a formal relationship. Once recognized, called by his personal name, and provided with a figurative stand-in, the spirit-as-person enters the realm of culture, the village. Vogel points out the following after she interviewed Baule men during a field study of Baule esthetics: "In commenting on the figures they were asked to rank, the Baule never used the particular 'It resembles a woman,' or 'It resembles a man,' but always the generic *sran*" (1980:4). They insisted, in other words, on the fundamental personhood of the figure.

Of all divinities, spiritual agencies, or fetishes, only *asiɛ usu* and men and women of the *blɔlɔ* are seen and represented in such personal human terms. The active, volitional aspect of their nature is what allows them to be perceived in terms of intentionality and personhood and thus differentiates them from other divinities or spirits.

God, *nianmien*, "does not play a very important role in Baule liturgical life" (Étienne 1976:34). Earth *(asiɛ)*, as we have seen, plays a far more important role in relation to

39. The sculptor Koffi Niamnien with two recently completed figures. Toumodi region, Côte d'Ivoire. 1981. Photograph by Lap Nguyen Tien.

village life and well-being, but although "called" through speech, addressed, and covenanted with, Earth remains a fundamental, organic power — a fixed essence or natural force. The other *amuin* are

> above all protective and vindictive divinities. They are vindictive in two ways, first by punishing (by sickness or death) those who attack their followers and, then, by punishing their own followers in the same way when they do not respect the ritual prescriptions of the cult.
>
> These protective and vindictive attributes generally interest the village community. One calls the fetishes to the village, one brings them out of their sanctuary for a procession around the village, one invokes them for collective ill-being (famine, epidemics, fire, flood, etc.). Vindictiveness is also manifest collectively (Étienne 1976:32).

"The relationship between fetishes and people is ambiguous" (ibid.:33), for although fetishes have powers that affect people, they are also highly dependent on people. Also, although supernatural, it is believed that they have no special abode other than nature in general, and their power can only be channeled when it is captured and attached to a material object. The idea is of an abstract force, more mechanistic than personal. Ancestors are also conceived of as persons, but they are invoked through an altar composed of the stools or chairs they used in their lifetime; they are already "known" and their existence in the *blɔlɔ* does not require any new personification.

Having discussed the similarity of "personhood" in both *asiɛ usu* and the Other-World mates of the *blɔlɔ*, differences should also be mentioned. One dissimilarity between the beings is that in one case, *blɔlɔ,* the living person is linked to only one Other-World person (always of the opposite sex). In the other case, *asiɛ usu*, it is not uncommon for a living person to be linked to a family or a male/female couple. In Lafargue's translation of a Baule account of the "birth of a Komyen," for example, one finds

> they were reassured that they had nothing to fear, for their son was going to come back with an *asiɛ usu* and become a *komiɛnfwɛ*. While waiting, his parents were to have made for him a small figure in wood *(waka sran)*, representing the male *asiɛ usu*. As for the female *asiɛ usu*, the new *komiɛn* himself would take care of it (1970:24).

Furthermore, inherent in the idea of *asiɛ usu* is the belief that these spirits live in families.

> Earth-spirits always live in society, in villages. They are sexual beings who marry and who reproduce....

> Most often, the [figure of the *asiɛ usu*] will soon be joined by a male or female companion, for they cannot live as celibates (Guerry 1972:104).

A relationship that is established between an *asiɛ usu* and a human being often outlives the person. Should a *komiɛn* die, it is said that the spirit looks within the family "for another horse to mount." It is as though the two families (real and supernatural) are linked in an ongoing, productive alliance.

The Other-World man or woman is a solitary individual linked to only one human being. I have written elsewhere (1980:3) that it is significant that the Baule never use the words "husband" *(wun)* or "wife" *(yi)* in relation to the

40. STANDING MALE FIGURE
Wood and paint. Height: 34.5 cm. FMCH 94.17.6. *Anonymous gift.*

41. STANDING MALE FIGURE

Wood and paint. Height: 32.4 cm. National Museum of African Art, Smithsonian Institution. Anonymous gift. (Alternative view may be found on page 3.)

42. STANDING MALE FIGURE

Wood and paint. Height: 27.5 cm. FMCH 94.17.4. Anonymous gift. (Alternative views may be found on pages 43 and 48.)

Other-World person. He or she is always referred to as the Other-World man or Other-World woman; in other words, the association is a dyadic sexual relationship, rather than the polyvalent marriage relationship that links two families in a web of mutual obligations. There is an actuality to this relationship that situates it in the immediacy of lived experience. Unlike the pre-existing reality of nature and the received or given ontology of the natural world, the *blɔlɔ* is a world that is revealed suddenly and experienced authentically: the palpable passion of a male/female relationship. The living partner admits to being "desired," in fact "demanded," by an invisible, sexual being.

The *blɔlɔ* mate, as understood by the living counterpart, is seen as a real-life lover. This may explain the twentieth-century depictions of the "personhood" of the *blɔlɔ* mate as a representation of a contemporary person — urbane, cosmopolitan, and truly "with it." Admittedly, the twentieth century has had a profound impact on Baule society. Since colonization on the eve of World War I, and since the integration of Baule culture into a world society, although Baule ideas of human beauty have remained fairly constant, the effects of Western fashion have influenced the Baule, as well as their depictions of Other-World men and women (cf. Ravenhill 1980:passim). This is not surprising, since the Other World has always been seen as parallel to the real world.

During the early colonial period, figures that represented Other-World men were often depicted with European headgear: pith helmets (Figs. 40 and 48), military caps *(képis)*, or hats. The elaborate male hairdos of former times became less common. Later, new hairstyles were depicted, as seen in the sculpted and parted hair of modern figures (Figs. 15, 41, and 42). A full range of fashionable clothes has been represented: shirts and ties, shorts and sandals, suits and long trousers, shoes or high heels. Female figures are also represented in modern fashion, but less often than male figures.[7]

Recent interpretations of bodily volume have changed most significantly in the depiction of the waist, a concept

43. STANDING MALE FIGURE
Wood and paint. Height: 38 cm. FMCH 94.17.1. *Anonymous gift.*

A Pair

Figures of a couple carved from a single block are very rare, but like pairs of free-standing Baule figures they probably represent the nature spirits known as *asiɛ usu*. We have independent proof of this assumption for this couple from Susan Vogel, who showed a photograph of it to Baule informants who confirmed that they "must represent nature spirits" (Roy 1985:61). They may well have been owned by a *komiɛn* diviner.

Since either men or women can become *komiɛn* diviners, it would be interesting to know whether there is any tendency for a diviner's figure to be of the opposite sex. In other words, did this figure belong to a male diviner and is that why the female figure is predominant and the male figure seems to play a supportive role?

The seated posture of this pair can be juxtaposed with Susan Vogel's observation that for *asiɛ usu* "The figure is described as the *asiɛ usu*'s 'stool' because the figure 'sits on it but can come and go'" (1977:168-69).

44. SEATED MALE AND FEMALE FIGURES

Wood. Height: 39cm. University of Iowa Museum of Art, The Stanley Collection. Photograph by Randall Tosh.

45. Front view. Photograph courtesy of the University of Iowa Museum of Art.

Details

46. *Detail of Figure 53, page 47.*

47. *Detail of Figure 15, page 20.*

48. Profile view of Figure 51, page 44.

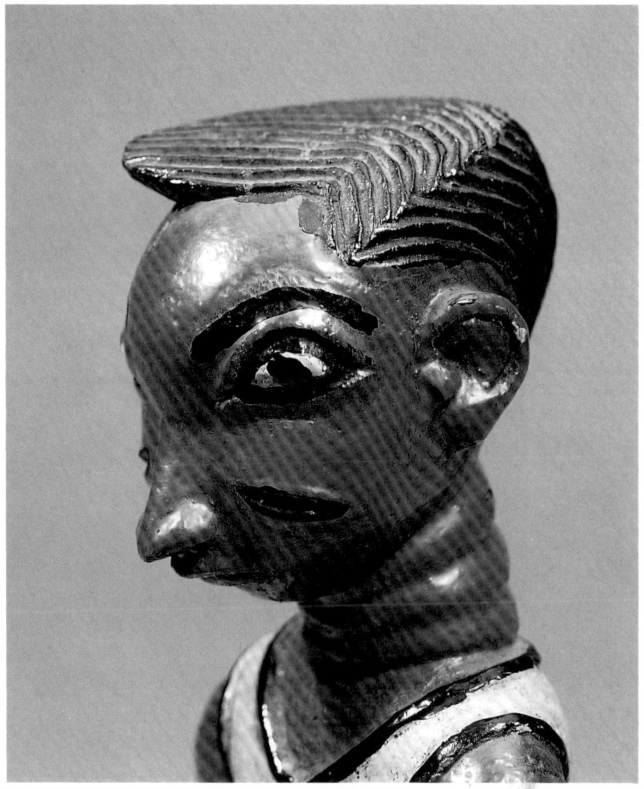

49. (Top) Detail of Figure 42, page 38.
50. (Bottom) Detail of Figure 14, page 20.

51. STANDING MALE FIGURE
Wood, glass beads, fiber. Height: 32.5 cm. National Museum of African Art, Smithsonian Institution. Anonymous gift. *(Profile view may be found on page 43.)*

borrowed from foreign fashion. Skin tones of light, dark, and red — formerly achieved with dyes — are now rendered with industrial paints.

The Other World continues to evolve. The entire gamut of twentieth-century fashion can be found in Baule figures. The Other World is indeed as immediate and responsive as the real world.

Conclusion

The attempt to translate another culture is never entirely satisfactory. The gaps of experience and knowledge seem insurmountable. Between the world as I have experienced it — as a Euro-American male of the mid-twentieth century — and the world as experienced by Baule men and women in their betwixt-and-between reality of tradition and modernity, how does one begin to explore empathetically the culturally defined, lived experience? To reflect — humanly, one hopes — on the experience of others, one must begin with the exegesis of their cultural concepts, the particular ways that words define the world and constitute social reality.

MacGaffey, in his study of "The Personhood of Ritual Objects: Kongo *Minkisi*" (1990:46), argues that

> Neither the thingness of an object nor the personhood of people is given in nature; both are the results of a local, culturally specific labeling process requiring, in each case, that a particular concept or status be intentionally recognized, that an apt candidate for the role exists, and that the status be assigned to the candidate by an approved procedure.

In his exploration of Kongo cosmology and concepts, MacGaffey points out that

> The most obvious external sign of the personification of *minkisi* is that they are invoked as *willful beings*.... [M]any of the obligations incumbent upon

52. Shop of an art dealer showing replica figures (colon) *inspired by clothed Baule figures. Dakar, Senegal. 1983. Photograph by Philip Ravenhill.*

those who come into contact with a *nkisi* have the effect of insisting that it be treated as though it were a person (emphasis added; 1990:53).

There are direct parallels here to the Baule concepts of *asiɛ usu* and the Other-World mates of the *blɔlɔ*, although perhaps, if I read MacGaffey correctly, the Baule cosmology may be even more insistent that the personhood of these spirits pre-exists their actual representation in figurative form. The creation of the form is a material recognition of the existential *personhood* of these spirits, willful beings who choose to impinge on human existence. They, too, are people *(sran mu)* who want to be greeted, to be lodged, to be fed, to be involved in a lasting relationship. The figure, *waka sran*, is a constant reminder of the supernatural "person" who exists in a special relationship to *me*. Through the figure the self acknowledges the other.

Notes

1. The literature on Baule culture and art is voluminous. Interesting aspects of Baule history, culture, and art are to be found in Weiskel 1980, Étienne 1972, 1976, Vogel 1973, 1977, 1980, 1988, and Ravenhill 1980 and forthcoming.

2. Cf. Étienne 1972 in which he discusses the collected writings presented for his doctorate.

3. Étienne defines *tukpɛ* as a "partner in institutionalized joking relationships between tribes, friends, comrades born the same year as Ego" (1976:72).

4. *Fwɛ* is an agentive suffix indicating "the one who does the action" (Carteron 1972).

5. The place of the *blɔlɔ* in individual Baule existence is more fully explored in my forthcoming book *Dreams and Reverie: Baule Images of Other-World Mates in the Twentieth Century.*

6. A collection of these miniature figures for necklaces is to be found in the collections of the Musée du Prophete near Vavoua in the central region of Côte d'Ivoire (cf. Ravenhill 1981).

7. On the concept of "clothed males" and "unclothed females" cf. Ravenhill 1980:17–18 and forthcoming, chaps. 2, 3, 4.

Bibliography

Carteron, Michel (R.P.)

1972 *Petit lexique baoulé - français.* Bocanda: Mission Catholique. Mimeographed.

Effimbra, Georges

1959 *Manuel de Baoulé.* Paris: Fernand Nathan.

Étienne, Pierre

1972 "Introduction." Thèse de troisième cycle. Paris (ORSTOM). Mimeographed.

1976 "Le fait villageois baoulé." In: *Communautés rurales et paysanneries tropicales. Travaux et Documents de l'ORSTOM,* No. 53:27–91.

Guerry, Vincent (R.P.)

1972 *La vie quotidienne dans un village baoulé.* Abidjan: INADES.

Lafargue, Fernand

1970 "La naissance d'un 'Komyen'." *Bulletin de Liaison.* Centre Universitaire de Recherches et de Developpement, Université d'Abidjan, pp. 21–25.

MacGaffey, Wyatt

1990 "The Personhood of Ritual Objects: Kongo *Minkisi.*" *Etnofoor* 3(1):45–61.

Pietz, W.

1985 "The problem of the fetish." *RES* 9:5–17.

Ravenhill, Philip

1980 *Baule Statuary Art: Meaning and Modernization.* Working Papers in the Traditional Arts, No. 5. Philadelphia: Institute for the Study of Human Issues.

1981 "Le musée du prophète Djouman Mihin, Vavoua, Côte d'Ivoire." *Godo-Godo.* Revue de l'Institut d'Histoire, d'Art et d'Archéologie africains, Université d'Abidjan 6:128–43.

1993 *Dreaming the Other World: Figurative Art of the Baule, Côte d'Ivoire.* Washington, D.C.: National Museum of African Art, Smithsonian Institution.

forthcoming *Dreams and Reverie: Baule Images of Other-World Mates in the Twentieth Century.* Washington, D.C,: Smithsonian Institution Press.

Roy, Christopher D.

1985 *Art and Life in Africa: Selections from the Stanley Collection.* Iowa City: The University of Iowa Museum of Art.

Vogel, Susan

1973 "People of Wood: Baule Figure Sculpture." *Art Journal* 33(1):23–26.

1977 Baule Art in the Expression of a World View. Ph.D. diss., New York University.

1980 *Beauty in the Eyes of the Baule: Aesthetics and Cultural Values.* Working Papers in the Traditional Arts, No. 16. Philadelphia: Institute for the Study of Human Issues.

1988 "Baule Scarification: The Mark of Civilization." In Arnold Rubin (ed.) *Marks of Civilization: Artistic Transformations of the Human Body,* Los Angeles, UCLA Museum of Cultural History, pp. 97–105.

Weiskel, Timothy C.

1980 *French Colonial Rule and the Baule Peoples: Resistance and Collaboration.* Oxford: The Clarendon Press.

Publication Presentation

Daniel R. Brauer *Design*
Irina Averkieff *Editing*
Denis J. Nervig *Photography (unless otherwise indicated)*
Anthony A.G. Kluck *Map Design*

Design and editing were accomplished on Macintosh computers using Aldus Pagemaker 5.0 and Adobe Illustrator 5.5. Type was set in Monotype Perpetua and Bodega Sans Old Style.

53. STANDING MALE FIGURE
Wood, paint, and beads. Height: 33 cm. FMCH 94.18.1. Anonymous gift.
(Detail view may be found on page 42.)